AWAKEN

2

BETTER

CHOICES

An Acronym Book For Our Emotions

Marquetta Marie

AWAKEN 2 BETTER CHOICES
An Acronym Book For Our Emotions

U.S. Copyright © 2021 No.

Published 2021 by Maquetta Marie

All rights reserved. No portion of this book may be reproduced, photocopied, stored, or transmitted in any form-except by prior approval of the publisher.

Unless otherwise noted, all Scripture quotations are taken from the King James Version of the Bible.

Printed in the United States of America

ISBN-13:978-1-7369699-0-8

Table of Contents

1 - Anger 8
2 - Alone 10
3 - Anxious 12
4 - Betrayed 14
5 - Bitter 16
6 - Broken 18
7 - Crushed 20
8 - Critical 22
9 - Doubt 24
10 - Defeat 26
11 - Embarrassed 28
12 - Empty 30
13 - Fearful 32
14 - Furious 34
15 - Grief 36
16 - Hurt 38
17 - Irritated 40
18 - Jaded 42
19 - Lost 44
20 - Mad 46
21 - Neglected 48
22 - Overwhelmed 50
23 - Pain 52
24 - Perplexed 54
25 - Quarrelsome 56
26 - Resentful 58
27 - Sad 60

28 - Sorrow	62
29 - Stuck	64
30 - Tense	66
31 - Worry	68
Letter to the reader	74
Contact	76

Greetings today, Awesome Reader,

I am so elated that you decided to invest in yourself and make this purchase. You are amazing, and you decided to enhance your communication skills more, guaranteeing to strengthen your relationships with others as you mature and evolve. This book was created with maturation in mind focusing on emotions and communication. Being that we were created for relationships, they take hits from our birth to our death. It's our job to see the attacks that formulate from the enemy and be able to effectively maneuver through the emotions that would cause destruction. We can all collectively gather more tools to place within our toolboxes to ensure we are reaching milestones successfully. Let's prepare to do life together because we have a plethora of lives to impact for the Kingdom.

Your Sister in LOVE,
Marquetta Marie

AWAKEN TO BETTER CHOICES

Awaken/ Greek- Exupnizo - no longer dull in sleep but up and revived to work

Diagregoreo - to keep awake, be on guard, being watchful to work

Awaken/ Hebrew - yaqats - to be stirred internally being awakened ready for action

quts/qus - excited unto explosion for an expelling of emergence

So why should we awaken?
When we awaken, we get up, becoming aware, being alert, having the knowledge to make change and impact.

When we awaken, we are able to shift the movement and momentum in our lives from what was to what is and shall be.

When we awaken now, the light is turned on; and what we were ignorant and in darkness beforehand get a shift and can walk in and walk out with knowledge.

When we awaken, the awareness allows us to observe critically both inward and outward so we deal with our issues so we can heal and be successful.

When we are exposed to something new, we are challenged to accept it so we can then change, or sadly we reject it and remain the same.

People oftentimes experience cycles/ circles in life having the same scenario or pattern of repeatedly experiencing stagnation which is discouraging.

Cycle/ The repetitive wheels in our lives, either positive or negative

Contamination
Yields
Calamity that
Leaves you
Empty

Cycles have a pattern: (NEGATIVE)

1- Encounter = you are faced with something
2- Emotion = Feeling from what you just faced
3- Experience = Calculations of encounter coupled with emotions being repeated
4- Environment = Surroundings or Conditions we live in and operate from in Life

Cycles have a pattern: (POSITIVE)

1- Encounter- Face to Face with a person, place, or thing, and events transpire
2- Emotion- You experience emotions in excess to gain an understanding of the encounter
3- Experience- What will you formalize holding to as TRUTH from your emotions
4- Expression- Articulate your feelings, go to the person and have a conversation
5- Enrichment- Learn the Lesson, Improve Self, Enhance Life moving forward
6- Environment- Your surroundings from your balanced perspective in Life

ANGER

Already

Not able to

Glean from

Each others

Response

Anger is a barrier from people being able to engage in effective communication. When we are angry, the defensive walls rise up against who we are in communication with. If you feel the need to defend yourself, your mind and mood will switch to that of by any means necessary mode. We will yell, scream, curse and lose control to the brink of fighting during times of anger. This is not righteous anger. If we can be real and honest, we lose it as we lose ourselves due to anger which is dangerous. When we lose control or lose ourselves and the emotions, we have take over us, we need to stop, pause, regroup and think. At this moment, we need to disengage and take a moment to breathe and think about processing the issue. Anger is a normal emotion that will come when we feel ignored, mistreated, taken advantage of, or not valued. Anger means you haven't set healthy boundaries and expressed your expectations from the start. No relationship is perfect or problem-free, but we can't solve problems in anger. Breathe, relax, calm down, and re-engage when you are able to express yourself properly and not lose your peace.

Prayer:

Father, we all experience anger at some point in our lives, but we want to be able to think clearly to get resolve. We understand that anger will cloud our judgment, so we ask that you stabilize our minds and settle our emotions. Father, you said you would give us victory, so let not our emotions get us nor let our minds cause us to be gotten by the actions of others. Help us to see issues with an open mind and open heart so you can come in and occupy the space bringing us solutions. Blow on our hearts and minds so we will think and act differently each time the test of anger is presented to us. Allow us to take a stand in you, so we don't lose our ground nor stumble on this path; oh, GOD in Jesus' name, we pray.

Amen

ALONE

Atmosphere

Lowers

Optimism

Narrowing

Expectations

When you feel alone, you then create a defense barrier to protect yourself. You can be isolated or around others, but you feel void and empty. This is not a good feeling, and sometimes it's a struggle to express this to others. We must own our feelings and then deal with our feelings because this is stemming from somewhere. An experience has hindered your ability to fully embrace those around you and be embraced as well. We were created for relationships, and being alone is not a part of the original design or intent. Different things can cause you to be alone or feel alone. Never feel bad for reaching out to people remembering we were created to participate in healthy relationships. Great connections via friends and family exist, so don't be fooled by negative experiences that now attack your mind and heart. Drop the walls and believe that since you are an amazing person, you will draw in the same people around you.

Prayer:

Father, we can't be alone when we truly have knowledge of you being everywhere. You are omnipresent, so there is no space you aren't already occupying. We just need to ask you to allow us to feel your presence. We remind you that you said you would never leave us nor forsake us, so father, we need you. We stand on that word knowing if you said it, then that settles it, father. As we draw nigh unto you in prayer, we ask that you draw nigh unto us, allowing us to draw closer unto you. Let us not fall for the deceptive seeds the enemy tries to plant in our mind, heart, spirit, and atmosphere. You are with us leading the way, so allow your presence to comfort us as you give us strength to move forward on this journey in life in Jesus' name, we pray.

Amen

ANXIOUS

Accumulation of

Negativity internally

e**X**aggerates

Issues

Objecting and

Underminng

Success

We have all experienced the overwhelming feeling of being anxious. An event or situation has had us on edge with our minds going millions of miles per millisecond. We don't even weigh or judge the thoughts to see what is valid and what is a stretch of our imagination. We think, and we overthink, but we should not let thoughts cripple us. Some things we can never stop from occurring, so plan accordingly and continue to move forward. We don't know all the answers despite the step-by-step instructions we try to create for ourselves. We can make a plan, but things can change on the spot and cause us to have to adapt. Be able to think critically and efficiently in life. Do not stay stuck in thoughts. Shift the thoughts to actions. Each day is a day to handle what we are able to in the renewed strength of our father. When we are anxious, it will lead to worry, and they both will overwhelm us with fear. When things work in opposition of you going forth and forward, you must deal with it.

Prayer:

Father, you told us to be anxious for nothing but for us to be thankful and always pray. We will cast our cares upon you because you care and have a solution. We will not be overwhelmed, so we give the weight of this burden unto you, father. Help us to solve the issues before us and allow us to hold unto the peace that you have released upon us. We need knowledge in this situation to help us better understand as we walk out your plan. You went before us and prepared the way, so give us strategy, so we don't get off track and lose our way. Allow us to have peace in knowing we don't have to do this alone. As we partner with your word and pray, we shall manifest everything on earth your word has said we can possess. We set our hopes in you, oh Lord, and we trust you father in Jesus' name we pray.

Amen

BETRAYED

Burdened by

Emotions

Tainted, Torn and

Ruined

Afflicting a

Yearning to

Evolve pass

Debilitating discomfort

Sometimes a person we place confidence in can betray us, and we repeat this offense in both heart and mind. The act plants a seed, and we do not get free if we don't deal with and heal from this place. The enemy uses betrayal to keep us from getting close to people because he knows two are better than one. We are created for relationships, and betrayal causes our hearts to harden towards others forcing isolation. Isolation leads to depression and causes us to suffer in silence, feeling people cannot be trusted. This is a weight you need to release to God because that burden is too heavy, and he said his burden is light. Betrayal can make you bitter, which fights against you becoming better or the best in relationships being stuck on past pain. You must heal, and we need to heal for real. They may have hurt you, and it was unsettling and stung to the core, but you are yet alive with breath so take your life back. You don't have to do life alone either; people can be trusted, and as you heal, you will be able to connect with covenant people.

Prayer:

We don't get to skip events of life, just being connected and close to you, oh God. As we go through experiences and situations helps us to get out of our emotions and be able to, in sober mind, see the big picture. Father, a false witness doesn't go unpunished, but we are to forgive the offender of the trespass. As we let go, then you have room to come in, and we need you, oh God. Some things are for the maturation of ourselves, and other things are to help us get keys to help others. We should learn from all situations and fully understand that what is before us will not always last. Father, as you are our strength and you bring us joy, help us to lean on you as we get through this. Let us not stay here but continue to press on because we still have work to do. Father undergird us and help us get from this place we are in now to a better place ahead in Jesus' name, we pray.

Amen

BITTER

Buried

Issues

Tackle

Triumph from

Ever being a

Reward

The enemy uses bitterness to fog our minds and cloud our judgment. We can't think of the present being stuck in the past due to it prohibiting us from going forward. Bitterness hits the least and the great not discriminating. Bitterness will plant seeds in our hearts and mind, so it's best to address pain immediately so nothing is rooted in us later. We can't live in the moment and experience joy being salty of what was in the past. We are not to be bitter, it's a slow venom that paralyzes joy and happiness. Things will not always go or look favorable, but we must be mature and resilient. Process what went wrong and make a plan and or regroup and do it again. We should learn lessons from setbacks and use these events to step up towards success. Don't let bitterness infiltrate your heart and mind because it's friendly with malice, offense, and delay, and it will cause great hindrance.

Prayer:

Father, we see wormwood trying to infiltrate the perimeters and contaminate our waters. Bitter water leads to a curse, and the cross breaks the curse for us, so we resist what has been removed. This problem will not stop us from becoming what you have spoken; oh God, we will get better from this. Let bitterness not take over the water that you have placed in our bellies that come from you. We reject wormwood; he can't occupy the throne of our mind. We give it to you, oh God. Let your light drive out darkness; light replace this bitterness with the sweet honey from above. Let love remove this bitterness that is trying to increase misery as you renew our life and soul. We will no longer speak death and bitter words, but we will speak life and live. Father heal us now so we can go to the next places we need in Jesus' name we pray.

Amen

BROKEN

Barriers that

Remain

Obstruct

Kind

Exchanges among the

Nations (People)

When you are hurt, it causes defensive and offensive walls to go up. You are on edge and do not connect to others. You become an island to yourself, and then discord and division creeps in, preventing healing from occurring in a person's life. When we are broken, a breakthrough seems impossible. The agony and hurt begin to cloud our sight and thoughts, so all we see is what broke us, and we are consumed by what was and what has happened. We can't see a change or any logical way out from the situation that has occurred. We are not optimistic, and the enemy creeps in during our vulnerability. Lets not let negative things keep us in a bad place, repeating harmful thought processes and being secluded and stagnant. We can give our brokenness to our father, and he will give us beauty for our brokenness.

Prayer:

Father, the silver cord must be broken off us that causes diabolical connections to come in. Break ties with us to pain, hurt, agony, affliction, and other things that leave us broken. Let the idols of life be broken, oh God, so nothing prohibits the healing and wholeness we need from you. Give us peace as you put together our pieces. Heal our broken heart and heal our broken spirit so we can get the beauty for ashes as you burn the burden. Teach our hands to war so our praise unto you God will break the bows of steel. Break oppression off us so we can judge well, oh God. You said you draw nigh to the brokenhearted, and you then save their spirit. As the scripture is fulfilled, let us hear you and have joy and gladness in Jesus' name.

Amen

CRUSHED

Carrying

Residue lacking

Understanding

Showing

Hurt

Expressing

Defeat

We feel crushed when we become disappointed by an unmet expectation from a person or thing. If things don't play out how you envisioned, it's ok; take that vision to the creator and revise it. We make plans, and our heavenly father smiles as they unknowingly then shift. When expectations are not met, or we experience pain or discomfort from a person, we hold on to that feeling. When things shift or go left from our plan, we need to stop and pray. There is a master plan for us created by our heavenly father. When we are in alignment, our soul and spirit won't be easily disrupted by things of this earth. We need to normalize taking things to God in prayer. We are to pray without ceasing, and prayer releases insight. We can't be crushed being blindsided if we prayed so God could highlight things for us. He would give us strategy when and if we submit, surrender, and supplicate. We may not understand his plan but following it will allow our lives to be blessed.

Prayer:

We understand, Father, that the crushing produces the oil, but the crushing doesn't feel good. Father, as you stretch our minds and increase our capacity to understand, sustain us in that place. The oil is made from you, our father, and the apothecary is both holy and anointed, so we are settled. The city of confusion and calamity is broken down when your oil runs down on us from our heads to our feet. Dip us in you, oh holy one, dip us in you, oh precious one, revive us, father. Father, break the gates of brass and cut the bars of iron in response to you liberating us from this place. We find what we need in you as we seek you in these hard times, so as we seek you, let us find you in Jesus' name, we pray.

Amen

CRITICAL

Condemning

Remarks

Inflict

Turmoil

Increasing

Continued

Affliction in your

Life

We are seeds that are planted in the soul of our innermost parts and in the soil of the ground or soil of air. If the seeds are negative as they are watered, they blossom into damaging stains in and on the soul. If the seeds are positive, they also will be watered and blossom into damaging stains in and on the soul. If the seeds are positive, they also will be watered and blossom into dynamic things. If you are super critical of yourself and others, then oftentimes, this stems from condemning remains from childhood or pain and trauma being repressed. When people experience things displeasing, often it's not discussed. If we begin to normalize expressing outwardly what we feel inward, communication will have a positive shift. We should not speak death resulting in more critical damage, but we can be candid and clear in communication to find resolve. Critical people lacked affirming and supportive words growing up, so their vocabulary and reach are minimal. What we lack in childhood is visible in adulthood when we interact with others. The negative opinions and rumors of others should not detail or debilitate your esteem. To shift this, you need to speak positively concerning yourself and others to shift the narrative.

Prayer:

Father help us to not be so critical but to respond in wisdom and love. We are a work in progress, but that's not an excuse for poor character. Potter, we are the clay, so make us and mold us as you have your way. We want to be love and give love, able to receive increase in areas we have lacked. As we grow in love, heal the hurt places we have that made us critical, so we respond differently to hurt people commanding a different response from them when we interact. Help us father in Jesus' name we pray.

Amen

DOUBT

Damaged

Outlook from

Unending

Battles in

Thoughts

A person who doubts everything is struggling to see the light of hope. Doubt places you in a disposition of darkness you can't exit alone. Doubt causes your faith to have blemishes and become damaged if it even exists at all. The seed of doubt is dangerous and needs to be plucked out immediately upon it being discovered. Negative thoughts will come to mind, but then you have a job to lift up truth to the lie. Doubt is a lie of worry exaggerated in excess, making you think no good escape exists. Have hope one minute at a time, and work at rebuking aerial attacks to your mind one thought at a time. Make a deliberate decision to believe again. Do not let doubt derange and destroy your faith.

Prayer:

Father, we know that there are levels to faith, so we ask that you help us get from level to level. We will not be shaken by the enemy that uses doubt to fight against our faith. We make an effort in hard times even now to not doubt father but to trust you and lean on you, not our shallow understanding. We do not know anything outside you sharing insight with us, so help us even now, father, so we can pass this test and ones to come. We walk by faith and not by sight, so what's in our view currently is temporary, and we declare the best is yet to come. Your word in us helps us not to waver as you hear us crying out to you. Faith arises, and doubts decrease and are cast in the sea, so we forget about it. Father, your love and compassion fuels our faith as we know you are with us. We seek you and are sustained by the strength and righteousness of your right hand. Thank you, father, for your intervention in Jesus' name, we pray.

Amen

DEFEAT

Darkness

Enters

Fighting an

Exit 2 embrace

Alternative

Thoughts

Defeat is a mindset that comes to a person when they encounter a setback. One setback is not failure or defeat, so keep striving. Several setbacks aren't defeats either, so let's shift our minds. Success is the drive to keep pushing forward despite the opposition that is before you currently. We learn our strengths and weaknesses in the attempts of action we present trying to be successful. You are not defeated, so be defiant against the disturbance; and be deliberate in going towards destiny. We are not defeated because we are victorious overcomers, so do not forget what has been declared over your life. When our mind is made up to see things completely through, we have the ability to walk in victory. We have to decide to not be derailed by defeat but decide to keep pressing forward. Let your hope be fueled today so you can reach destiny with a clear mind as you rejoice.

Prayer:

Father, we know we have victory in you, so we will not allow defeat to settle in our hearts or mind. Father, we overcome by the blood of the lamb and the power of the testimony of Jesus, so we come against failure and all things trying to make us defeated. Father, you are our refuge and strength and our present help and only help truly in times of trouble. We thank you for victory in our lamb who was slain, and we will not forget and forfeit what you have spoken to us. We sing unto you a new song remembering the marvelous things you have done. Father, your right hand and your holy arm have brought us victory even now. We are born of you, so we overcome the world knowing our victory is in our faith in you. We trust you to bring us to a place of victory, destroying defeat in Jesus' name.

Amen

EMBARRASSED

Entered a
Moment
Being
Aware that a
Release was
Rejected
And Said to be
Silly
Stupid so you
End up feeling
Dogged out dissed

We are not perfect, so do not attempt to be as such. We can be silly, we can be human, we can make mistakes. Take the burden of perfection off your shoulders. Embarrassment is temporary; one moment or several moments are not the end all of life. Deal with the setback or the awkwardness and move forward. We conform to the norms of society but also know everyone will not be pleased by your actions or words. We are all different, we are unique, we are to be peculiar in our own design from God. Don't feel inadequate or invaluable due to being different or having an awkward experience. Things happen, so keep living because in that moment, you did not die. Moments will pass, so learn from it whatever is valuable and don't get caught slipping twice the same way. We live, and we learn, so all is not lost, but all is well.

Prayer:

Father, you are the author and finisher of our faith who has gone before us and prepared the way. You knew that this moment would arise, and you know that there is victory after this. Help us to hold our head up high and make it past this situation. We know defining moments of character are forged when we deal with a situation and allow us to heal ourselves from the situation. We have not because we haven't asked, so we ask for your intervention now in this situation. Help us, Lead us, guide us, comfort us, and show the way now in Jesus' name we pray.

Amen

EMPTY

Enter

Moments that you

Pour out

Then see nothing

Yielded back

Most times, people feel empty due to not seeing or feeling residual from their release. We do not give out to receive back, in regard to people owning us anything for being genuine. It does, however, feel good when people see you and appreciate you for what you bring into the equation. It is due to them pouring out but not being poured back into on a daily basis. We need balance, and we need wisdom in all our interactions. We should be willing to pour, help, give, release, and bless others beyond measure; when we give, we will receive; the word says it's more blessed to give than to receive. Time changes, seasons change, people change, things change. We must see with both our eyes looking both naturally and spiritually at the thing we experience and encounter. Relationships must be reciprocal; if not engage in conversation and if there is no change, you need to exit. Connect to people you can fill up, but they need to be able to pour back into you as well when needed.

Prayer:

Father, you said that we can drink from the well that never runs dry, so we ask you to fill us where we are empty. Father, we know that in you we can be filled, and when we leave, we will no longer be empty. Lord, we need you because right now, there is a void, and it is causing us pain. Help us to uncover the root of the emptiness so the void can be filled. As you help us and guide us through this, we will continue to seek your face knowing that we need you. We thank you and praise you in advance in Jesus' name.

Amen

FEARFUL

Failing to

Enter new

Arenas or

Realms

From

Understanding being

Lacked

People fear what they do not understand.
People fear what they can't pre-determine.
People fear what challenges their thoughts.
People fear what makes them uncomfortable.
People fear new things that require effort.
People fear failing or not being accepted.
Fear will make you stagnant, preventing purpose from being birthed.
Fear will paralyze your mind and body and cause momentum to cease.
Fear fights against the faith you have and has you stuck not wanting to do anything.
Be free in your mind from fear
Be free in your heart from fear
Be free in your soul from fear
Be free in your spirit from fear
Freedom comes from shifting your mindset
Freedom comes from deliberate change in thoughts.

Prayer:

Father, you haven't given us fear, but you have endowed us with power, love, and a sound mind. We understand that there is no fear in love; oh God, we ask that your perfect love begins to defend us against fear. Let your perfect love begin to tear up the tormentor coming for us to paralyze us and cause stagnation. Who you set free is free indeed, so we stand on the liberty of freedom that comes from you, oh Lord. You gave us authority to tread on the head of the enemy father so loose the bands of fear that are trying to choke us out. We bless you, risen King, and thank you for peace over this wind of fear being released. We submit ourselves to you, oh GOD knowing that fear must flee us because you cover us, oh Lord in Jesus' name.

Amen

FURIOUS

Feelings

Undermanaged

Released

In

Outrages instigate

Unnecessary

Situations

This emotion brings a few friends like rage, wrath, resentment, and anger. We begin to pop off and be short-fused when we lack the proper verbiage to articulate emotions. Everything will set you off when you are lacking the ability to express yourself properly. When you are furious, you might fight, undermine people, rebel, engage aggressively, and do some outrageous things because you are overwhelmed emotionally. Feelings are normal and should be embraced. Once you embrace them, be able to express them to others and then release them if they are negative. If you are furious, you don't think things out properly because your mind is captive by the thought or action that holds you in that set place. Breathe, think, talk, and release.

Prayer:

Help us father to articulate ourselves properly and be able to get resolve without causing damage and destruction. Father, you told us to be angry, so we can have emotions and express them, but you told us to sin not. Untangle us from any bondage that would cause us to shame your name due to us acting up in our flesh. Let our flesh not cause us to mess up the provision you have for us. We can't keep ourselves, but you are a keeper, so we ask you to help us and keep us gracious father in Jesus' name we pray.

Amen

GRIEF

Gloom	Gloom	Growing
Readily	Rises	Resistance
Increases	Inside	Inciting
Each day	Expelling	Erratic

      Fighting Freedom
      Feelings of hope
          Feelings

Grief puts you in a prison of sadness and distress as it chokes the life out of you very slowly. No one likes to lose a loved one because the separation from death stings. No one enjoys or embraces death because we do not understand it aside from knowing we can no longer enjoy the person's presence. We all deal with death differently, so we can't judge the grief process of the person, but we can wage war on the spirit of grief. We can't tell people how to grieve or how to feel, but we can interject with love through prayer and availability for the person. When we see depression, sorrow, or other feelings entering into the atmosphere. We must step in and try to help. Each person dealing with loss differently will have emotions that flood their mind. We can't be insensitive to their feelings and needs, but we can't let them grieve themselves to death or destroy their life. Prayer, love, and time is the only remedy during their healing process, and the duration can't be measured. Lift the person or yourself up in prayer. Be love or give love to the person in need and in distress. Do things to build some new memories, so they aren't repeating that hurt and pain over and over.

Prayer:

Father let grief not settle in our hearts or minds causing us pain that pulls us away from you and people. Let grief not consume our eyes and spirit, thus preventing us from meaningful relationships with people because of pain. Let bitterness, guilt, and resentment loose us now, so we aren't slaves to destruction in any way. This weight of grief is heavy; oh Lord, it overwhelms us and causes us to slip and become unbalanced. Father, we have no strength, and we ask for help in laying aside this weight that has beset us. Father, we give the weight to you knowing that you care about us, so we aren't alone. Take this hurt; we don't desire it any longer father, heal these wounds we have because of this situation. Have compassion for us, Father, according to your multitude of mercies as you strengthen us with your mouth in Jesus' name, we pray.

Amen

HURT

Have

Unbearable

Repeating

Thoughts

Hurt settles in the heart and the mind as it pollutes your spirit and atmosphere. Hurt places the painful experience on repeat in your mind, which alters your reality and damages your soul. Hurt prohibits you from letting the walls down and connecting to people. Hurt doesn't allow you to heal. Healing is the remedy for hurt, and that comes from God. When we are hurt, if we don't heal, it will bring other feelings or spirits. Hurt will bring pain, rejection, resentment, bitterness, and other feelings with it to affect you. When we are hurt, we need to acknowledge it, be willing to talk about it, carry it to God and let it go. Normalize being able to discuss your feelings with others. Especially the ones who hurt you. Normalize after engaging with the people and or persons to then pray and release it so no residual remains. If the issue occurs again, maybe you need to release the people but never let the hurt remain.

Prayer:

Father, you said you desire that we prosper and be in good health even as our soul prospers. We believe that and stand on that word, knowing you can heal any hurt we feel currently. As we seek your heart, father, we ask that you heal us with your healing rain. Father, let your mercy increase over us as you heal us; we need a touch from you so we can breakthrough. We repent and ask for relief, so hurt doesn't turn into grief or a spirit of heaviness. When we hurt, we know you hurt due to you caring for us so much, oh God. Father, we ask that you send forth your angels like you did for Daniel to alleviate hurt and agony. Father, we ask that you condemn tongues that rise up and cause the whisperers to become silent. Father, we ask that you replace hurt and pain with healing so we can continue to move forward and not lose time, faith, or momentum. Father, give us peace as you heal us and give us knowledge to keep us from being hurt and destroyed in Jesus' name, we pray.

Amen

IRRITATED

Inciting of

Repressed

Release

Increases

Turmoil

And Agitation

That is

Expressed

Demeaningly

Irritation comes from annoyance and also frustration in life. The feelings are not bad but allowing them to settle and shift your mood is a problem. Communication will assist in alleviating what is bothering you, so be willing to talk. We must learn to let things out and not hold things internally, causing us turmoil. We can communicate effectively and release without being rude, disrespectful, or damaging to another person. Irritation, if not released constructively, can turn into resentment, bitterness, and anger that will open the door for offense. Irritation comes from many things stemming from annoyance and also frustration in our life. The feelings are not bad; we have feelings and need to express them on a continual basis. We must be intentional in not allowing our feelings to shift us as we settle in them. In order to bring resolve to any emotion and in order to move forward progressively, we have to communicate effectively.

Prayer:

Father, let irritation not bring frustration to the grace you have released upon our lives. Let irritation not frustrate our purpose in you and with our relationships with people. Father, you called us to be salt, meaning we add flavor to people and circumstances. Help our release to be seasoned in your grace and love. Help us to see things for how they are in spirit so we can remain sober in our mind and speech when the enemy comes to attack our emotions. We understand that none of the weapons against our emotions can stand if we yield ourselves to you, so help us now, father in Jesus' name, we pray.

Amen

JADED

Joy

Always

Derailed

Emptying

Delight

A jaded person has an inability to rejoice and have real joy because they are stuck on bad experiences. We are supposed to rejoice with those who rejoice and cry with those who cry. When people aren't able to have compassion due to things going erroneously in their lives, they become emotionless due to the root of them being jaded. They have had a plethora of experiences that haven't been good, and now they lack enthusiasm for themselves and others. This is a dangerous place to be in because this can open the door to envy, malice, jealousy, and contention. When you are jaded, you may feel internally that you deserve nothing, and people around you are undeserving of good things as well.

Prayer:

Father, help us to truly have a heart for people as you have a heart for them. Let us be able to show compassion and rejoice with people in their turn of entering a winning season. Let us rejoice and be glad when we see someone get the victory knowing you have no respect of persons. You didn't run out of blessings for us as you blessed one. You still have more, and if we learn to clap and be glad for others, we shall reap celebration as well. You will withhold no good thing from those who love you. We can't say we love, but house hate so heal us so we can walk in love and show emotions in a healthy manner in Jesus' name we pray.

Amen

LOST

Living

Outside the

Saviours

Territory for you

When we are in darkness, we have no direction, and we are lost. We are experiencing life outside of the will, way, and word of our creator. When we live outside the boundaries or guidelines he has for us, then trouble unfolds. We need to stay in the boundaries and lateral limits the father has predestined for us in life. It's better to abide in his will and his plan rather than do our own thing. When we go astray, we get behind the timeline and power curve of the move and momentum our father has for us. When we are lost, just pause and press in by way of the spirit through prayer. Prayer will release a signal that will allow us to be located and rescued so we can be realigned and restored.

Prayer:

Father, I know that you will never leave us, not forsake us, you will be with us until the end of the earth. You have come to seek and save that which has been lost, oh God. We rejoice knowing that you leave the ninety-nine for the one because you are an excellent steward and shepherd. We thank you that we all have value, and we all are the apples of your eye. We thank you that you have dispatched angels to help us, and you have given them charge over us to guide us and keep us from falling and failing. The enemy will have us isolated from others and lost where we stand, thinking if we are alone, he can devour us as he seeks to attack us. We are never alone, though, so strengthen us as the one so we can put a thousand to flight and cause the angels, all 72,000 that have been charged over us, to stand with us and fight. Father turn the light on so we can find our way, you said light drives out darkness, and we believe it, as we conceive it, to receive it and release it in Jesus' name, we pray.

Amen

MAD

Multiplied

Asinine thoughts

Disrupting your peace

When we are mad, we are being prevented from having any logical thoughts, which is very destructive. The irrational thoughts we possess cause a disturbance and disruption in our peace and sound mind. Everything begins to agitate us as irritation increases, and anything in our paths becomes an enemy we are ready to take out. We need to get our emotions in check at this point because anything spoken or acted on in this emotion will result in damage, sometimes being irreparable. When we are mad, we need to again be able to pause and calm ourselves down, allowing time to process and think so we can express ourselves and get resolve. You must be able to communicate your grievance and air out the way you feel about the person or the situation. When you are able to articulate yourself, you need to be mindful that the person you release to can receive or reject the conversation. If they receive it, then you will be able to have resolve, but if they reject it, then be free in being able to release the negative emotions and keep moving forward.

Prayer:

Father help us to weigh the emotions we feel so we can express ourselves with dignity. We do not want to sin against you or sin against one another. You told us to be angry but to not sin, so we need your help in abounding and abiding in your law. Our heart is wicked and deceitful, and the enemy would love for us to lose our testimony in this situation. Show us our fault in this as you mature us in this instance. Show us the hearts and minds of the other people in this situation so we can get a solution when we speak to them. We do not want to give room to the enemy to have victory in any area of our lives. Let our emotions not oppress us, causing us to be separated from wisdom, knowledge, and understanding. Strengthen us so we can take a stand but stabilize us so we don't lose ground in Jesus' name; we pray.

Amen

NEGLECTED

Nurture

Escaped your

Growth

Leaving you

Empty

Crushed

Tormented

Ensnared and

Delayed

Neglect truly hurts people to their core of existence because their foundation for life becomes unsettled. We are created for relationships, and the enemy hits our emotions by way of experiences to alter the relational design. Neglect hurts because the bonds you needed to build with people could not be forged and formed. Neglect leaves you broken in certain foundational emotional development because we don't grow past the place we couldn't grow from. We oftentimes stay stuck in that place because no one helped us keep reaching milestones for healthy relationships. When we miss stages in development, it leaves openings and gaps in our mind, emotions, heart, and spirit. These openings will be filled when you can identify the pain from neglect and then talk about it so healing can begin internal and be reflected external. You must understand that nothing about you caused anyone to neglect or reject you. You have to understand that you deserve to be treated with dignity and respect and also that love is your portion. Break the chains of neglect that sabotage your growth so you can reach every place the father has predestined you to reach.

Prayer:

Father, let us not neglect not the gifts you have placed in us spiritually due to neglect naturally. Father, you created us for relationship, and the enemy hits our life to derail emotional growth. We see him and expose him as we cast our cares upon you because you care for us. Heal us from neglect, oh Lord, and fill every gap and space with your healing and love. We are the apple of your eye, so we can lean in your arms and feel safe. Renew our hearts and mind as we find refuge in you and hide in you until the healing takes place. Let the past not prevent us from getting to purpose. Help us as we draw close to you in prayer, knowing that you will meet us where we are, oh Lord. Thank you for healing us and helping us to be able to move forward in a healthy manner in Jesus' name.

Amen

OVERWHELMED

Opportunities being
Viewed as an
Experience that
Ruins and
Worries your
Heart
Enclosing on your
Life
Making you
Experience
Defeat

We were given witty ideas and inventions to advance the Kingdom, and as a bonus, we are blessed from it. GOD will not place more on us than we are able to handle because he knows the breaking point, and his desire is not to overwhelm us and push us into caves and dungeons. He delights in us and desires we prosper and be in good health in our mind, heart, emotions, finances, businesses, and relationships. When we are overwhelmed, it's a sign we are doing things in our strength and not resting on GOD drawing strength from him. Yes, we work the vision because we need to put our hands to the plow, but the vision should not overwhelm you nor drown you. The vision is supposed to enhance life and walking and working in purpose is supposed to refresh you, not ruin you. Opportunities in and of GOD are never to be viewed as obstacles, so we have to refresh the sight before us through prayer. If the vision is from GOD and it builds the Kingdom, there may be opposition, but don't be overwhelmed; rest in knowing you overcome.

Prayer:

Father, we desire to be in the will of you and not in your way. Father, you said you would lead us and guide us, so we place the vision back in your hands. Father, you said to write the vision and make it plain, and by us having the vision, we would then be able to see. Father, help us to rejoice as you work it out for our good as we work. Father, we waited on you and stepped out in obedience, so we ask you to bless our Faith and enable us to finish this race. Father, you said when you are for us, you are more than anything that can try to stand against us. Father cause contention and opposition to bow at your strength and might. Father, our devotion will not run out as we keep seeking you throughout this process. We renew our minds in your word and look to you for peace as we go through this process in Jesus' name.

Amen

PAIN

Pollution

Attaches

Internally altering your

Navigation

Pain comes to paralyze you like you just like that spirit of fear, so you must rebuke pain. You will not have any progress or productivity if you stay in a polluted place. Pollution places a fog over our senses, so we can't see, hear, feel, or interpret correctly. When the fogged filter of pain begins to replace the filter of free flow agape, we run into problems. Pain pulls us apart from other people, preventing them from pouring into us because we can't receive from them. Pain shifts our perspective, and normally the shift is negative unless you heal past the pain. Pain feeds on betrayal, brokenness, hurt, bitterness, malice, neglect, rejection, and abandonment. Pain will use any emotion to feed off it negatively to cause you to spiral and isolate.

Prayer:

Father break the chains of fear and pain that is trying to overturn our life. We commit our life to your ways and declare that we shall walk in the fulness of the blessings you promised through covenant. Jesus took on the curse of pain, so it is not our portion, we don't have to hurt, but we are able to cast hurt unto you. You are a shield for us, and you are a lifter up of our heads, so we give to you what has attached itself to us. Heal us, father, as you touch us and cause us to have victory in every area that has caused us pain in our lives. Pain has a purpose to push us into prayer, and we get it, and we are coming to you, oh Lord. We won't stop pressing in prayer so take this pain away, oh God and all residue the enemy will try to have us recall. Help us to rebuke the recalled memories so they won't ruin us because you have us father in Jesus' name, we pray.

Amen

PERPLEXED

Problem
Entering
Rest due to the
Pull that
Lowers
Expectation causing
e**X**aminations that
Delay us

Why are you perplexed when the creator has gone before you and prepared the way. When we try to figure things out and lean on our understanding, we can begin to seed confusion in ourselves. Our master has the master plan, so why not pray and tap into his blueprint for your success. We can't look to others for the measures of success to unfold in our lives, but we must look to our father, the author, and finisher of our faith and our predestined way. When we get out of ourselves and get into prayer, the problem solver will come through. We don't have to sit idle and waste time trying to figure out every detail of the plan. We don't have to be vexed about what went wrong and try to perfect anything either because things never going perfectly according to our set plan, even if it is sealed by GOD. When we are at peace, our mind is at ease, and we are free. Break loose from the bondage of overthinking to the point of not being able to take any action.

Prayer:

We know you to be a waymaker, so we ask that you make a way in this situation. Father, help us to make the right choices and to rest in the vision you have established for us. We don't have to have sleepless nights due to not fully understanding the plan. You have gone before us and made the way, and you will release what we need each step of the way. Faith without works is dead so allow us to come alive with each step of obedience. We know that all things are working together for our good despite how we feel. We will acknowledge you, oh Lord, we will seek you, oh Lord. We place our hand in your hands, asking you to lead us and guide us and always stay beside us. Thank you for your grace being sufficient for us; oh Lord, in Jesus' name, we pray.

Amen

QUARRELSOME

Quickly
Undergoing
Arguments
Ruining
Relationship
Each time you
Lift up a
Sword to
Overtly destroy people with your
Mouth as you
Eagerly engage in conflict

No one takes pleasure in always interacting with a person who is miserable and quarrelsome. Everything is not a fight, and everything doesn't have to end in disagreement. You do not know everything and you being alive is a sign despite age that there is more to learn. It's okay to voice your opinion, and it's okay to express yourself but have balance so you can have peace. If people always leave your life, you need to evaluate yourself. If the only people who remain in your life are due to dependency, dear heart, you are the problem. Conflict is excellent, and it doesn't have to be avoided, but always finding problems and remaining in a negative state of mind and heart should be avoided. Quarrels will leave you always looking for issues in others so you can have an advantage to one up then, and no one really likes the one-upper.

Prayer:

Father allow the holy spirit to fall fresh on us each day. Father, we need to be free from the need to be right. Father, we need to be free from bickering and cantankerous seeds being planted in our lives. Father help us to be able to get along with people and be kind so we can reap kindness. Father give us insight on when it's necessary to go in and when we need to fall back and intercede. Father balance us with a sound mind, wisdom, a prayer life, and discernment. Father quarrels against people continuously will incite a spirit of killing and murder. Father always having quarrels shows we are weak in problem-solving and critical thinking. Father help us to forgive people seeing where they are, so we, in wisdom, can build them and enhance the relationship. Father, let us not be delivered into the hand of the enemy and open doors to pestilence to hit everything we touch. Father, we will not seek to avenge ourselves, causing your sword to be released upon us like in Leviticus. We pray today to resolve quarrels, act mature, drop offense, build relationships, and walk in love in Jesus' name.

Amen

RESENTFUL

Rudely
Express
Sentiments
Engulfed in
Negativity
That
Fosters
Undermining of
Loved ones

The enemy has a way of placing thoughts in our mind that then cloud our mind and affect our heart. He has us begin to evaluate all we feel we have done for someone and weigh their response and reactions to determine our worth. If they can't measure up to our expectations that we normally haven't told them about, we become resentful for the time, treasure, and talent released upon them. It's understandable to desire a person to give freely without bounds to you as you have to them, but if they don't, do not resent them. When relationships are amicable, you talk about healthy boundaries and also expectations, so there is no room for resentment. When you sacrifice and don't see it bringing dividends, you get resentful. When you pour out constantly, but people leave you empty, you feel resentful. When you go above and beyond for others, and there is no reciprocity, and you calculate where you could have been had you not supported them, it causes resentment. These are not good places to allow the mind to settle, so we need to submit these thoughts over the Lord. Yes, some people are manipulators, users, and abusers, but all are not like that, so deal with people according to the measure they have released, not from the residual of others.

Prayer:

Father, I do not desire to displease you, so I ask that you come into my heart and mind and help me. Father, I have calculated all the things I have done, and I harbor resentment in my heart and mind for not being acknowledged, appreciated, and valued. Father, I am angry that the release given was not reciprocated, and I don't feel satisfied with the results before me. Help me to feel love and support so I can heal and grow out of the calculative habits I have created. I am safe to be a giver and give with a cheerful heart, even if things are reciprocated. Father, you keep score, seeing all things and knowing all things, so you reward in your time, father. Give me peace as you settle and establish me oh God in Jesus' name, I pray.

Amen

RESTLESS

Repetitive
External
Situations
That
Lock and
Ensnare our
Soul and
Spirit

When we are restless, we are unable to find peace in our circumstances which feeds worry. Our father is our peace, and we are required to rest in that knowledge. The enemy comes to steal our peace which causes us to rest, and he replaces it with restlessness. Take a deep breath in and blow out the negativity that has crept in unaware, causing unrest in your body and mind. Take a moment to close your eyes and be able to envision you accomplishing the goal at hand. As you see yourself doing what needs to be done, find rest. If you can see it, then write it out and achieve it because there are no limits or bounds to your success. If you have a vision and have written out the plan, there is no need to be restless. If you have sought the face of the father and heard him clearly, no need to be restless.

Prayer:

Father, we know that you cause the weary to find rest, and in that rest, you release peace. Father, we are set out to accomplish the vision, but we don't want to be restless and unsatisfied unable to do anything. Father, as we pray, we ask that you refresh us while you restore and repair us. As we seek your face, oh God, there is an exchange that transforms us. We believe in your word, oh GOD, and we enter into your rest, father. In your rest, we find healing; in your rest, we find prosperity; in your rest, we find strength; in your rest is the peace of our righteousness sown. We thank you for rest and peace overflowing in our lives in Jesus' name.

Amen

SAD

Sorrow

Abides in your

Dwelling place

When we are sad, it causes us to come to a low state of mind. We are unable to see the good or recall our minds to the positive things. We have to then decide to walk in Joy because it is a gift given to us from our father. Walking in Joy positions you to receive the outpour and fresh anointing to conquer the day. Joy releases a sound and sight to those you encounter, and then they desire to partake in Joy as well, causing a shift.

Prayer:

Father, we come against this spirit of sadness trying to cause us grief. We will not allow our minds to be altered due to the enemy trying to creep in on us. We submit our emotions to you, asking you to help us navigate through this. We meditate on you, father, so our thoughts can be sweet, breaking the chains of sadness. We remember the good things you have done for us in times past, oh GOD, and we make ourselves glad thinking of your goodness. Father, we ask you to cause our flesh to rest in you as we rejoice and give you glory for making us glad. Thine is the Kingdom and the power, and we thank you for the shift now in Jesus' name we pray.

Amen

SORROW

Sadness

Overwhelms you

Rising over

Returning to an

Overcoming

Winning Stage

Sorrow is a deep overwhelming sadness that begins to flood you, and you drown in it. These feelings leave you unsatisfied and hopeless, ushering you into depression. Sorrow causes us to dwell in the low places and valleys for too long, not having an exit from now to the next. Sorrow is sadness increasing to the point of overwhelming you causing you to feel defeated and in despair. Sorrow sings songs of depression over you, so you stay in a warped mindset as it destroys your atmosphere. You can't dwell in sorrow mixed with guilt and sadness any longer due to life circumstances. You need to live and get up because you have more work to do.

Prayer:

Father exchange our garment of sorrow for a garment of gladness, so we complete our race with grace. Father, what the enemy is trying to use to divert us and drag us into sorrow, we ask you to destroy. We declare we shall see the victory on this side, oh Lord as you cause us to overcome. We declare that as we praise, it will confuse the enemy, and he will back up and be shut up. We declare that we are rejoicing in anticipation of the good things to come. We thank you for being GOD and give you the glory, praise, and honor that is due unto you in Jesus' name, we pray.

Amen

STUCK

Shallow

Thoughts

Undermine

Coming into

Knowledge

When we think small, we live small from the measure of Faith acquired in our belief. The mind packs power, and where it goes, our lives follow. When we can see something, it enables us to be able to conceive it as we thrust forward. We are to have progression in our lives, and we are to see growth. When we have expectations that are exceeded, it stirs up our Faith in our father and causes him to move on our behalf even more. When we are stuck, the enemy will tell us we are forgotten and overlooked by our heavenly father causing us to doubt and possibly lose faith. We are to see value in all we do and know we were created for a purpose. If we are stuck, then there is an issue with us getting in position so we can help others get into place. What derails us also delays others because we are interconnected despite how we feel about others. This is why we need to love people so we can desire to see them win, understanding victory and success is corporate not just for one but all.

Prayer:

The word tells us that deep cries out unto deep so as we pray remove us from shallow banks to deep waters. Father, we are not wise in our own eyes, but we look to you for knowledge, understanding, and wisdom. We may think we know the way, but we humble ourselves and ask you to show us the way. Be the lamp unto our feet and the light for our path, oh GOD, so we will not be stagnant but be able to see production as we move forward in Jesus' name; we pray.

Amen

TENSE

Trying to

Enter a

New place but

See no

Exit

We are not to be stressed or tensed concerning anything we encounter or experience in life.

Prayer:

Father, your yoke is easy, and your burden is light, so we ask you to help us even now. We release this tension to you, asking you to help us find peace in our process. We trust the plan you have given us, and we will wait on you for instructions each step of the way. Father, you are our help that we can look up towards, knowing you are above us, overlooking us. Thank you for your hand being in our lives and giving us a way to escape in you. We set our hopes in you, knowing that you will remove the tension and enable us to trust you more in Jesus' name, we pray.

Amen

TROUBLED

Try to
Rise
Over
Unseemingly
Bad
Life
Encounters but have
Difficulty

We are not going to avoid troubles in life just because we made GOD the head of our lives. When opposition comes, it's an opportunity for obstacles to be obliterated. Trouble is not to take you out; it should be to strengthen you as you see the might and strength of GOD. The testimonies we develop help to build our faith as we learn the truth about our heavenly father. When we are aware that each time we begin to take off, something restricts us or hinders us, we need to pray. When you are alerted to attacks that arise in your life, causing ruin to success, you need to strengthen your relationship with GOD. When people begin to come for you and you are under attack, you need to go and pray. The adversary sees more by way of spirit than we do, so we need to be in the presence of our father so we can combat his cohorts and conquer everything sent to crush us.

Prayer:

Father, we bring our troubles to you knowing that you are a problem solver. We ask you to undergird us as we cry out to you, father. We ask that you show us the way as you make the crooked places straight in our lives. We ask for an increase in peace, so even our enemies will be at peace with us. We know that no weapon formed against us can prosper, so we come to you, so we don't mess up what you have set up. Trials come to make us strong, and if the enemy is fighting against us, then it's because elevation is here. Weeping may endure for a night, but we know Joy is coming in the morning. Lead us and guide us through these tests and enable us to please you as we stand strong in Jesus' name; we pray.

Amen

WORRY

When

Outcomes

Replay

Repetitively as

You try to do anything

We were not created to worry, but we were created to worship. When we worry, we are giving worship to the cares of life and focusing on the problems being larger than they truly are at all. When we decide to worship GOD, we place him as the biggest thing in our life, making everything else small in comparison to him. We need help from the creator in order to make an impact at any level. As we begin to worship our father, he brings us peace as he enters into our life storm. Prayer and relationship will root out all worry because you then know that GOD has heard you, and you begin to feel comforted. Worry can not continue to be a stronghold that seduces you into being stagnant.

Prayer:

Father, we will not let the cares of this world deceive us and cause us to worry, thus becoming unfruitful. Let us worship you when worry tries to hit us, so we are refreshed in your presence. No one lives a life that is problem-free, but we can find solutions to anything we encounter when we submit to you and supplicate. Father, when we have issues, we are to bring them to you so you can cleanse our heart and mind and work on our behalf. We believe you can do anything but fail, and we trust you to come through for us because you are sovereign, oh GOD, in Jesus' name, we pray.

Amen

Dear Awesome Reader,

You have made it to the end, and I hope we were able to enhance your toolbox. Knowledge is power, and now you have some keys to help you unlock some things. These are a few of the emotions that we go through on a day-to-day basis in life. The emotions are not bad due to them causing us to feel. However, we must handle the responses from the emotions appropriately. It is my hope and desire that you have been able to identify with these emotions and that you will be able to release better responses. It is one thing to enter a situation and be unaware of what's coming against you; in these cases, your success might not be easily obtained. When you have weapons of warfare, and you are able to identify them with previous knowledge, you come out a winner in the fixed fight. Remember, the weapons of our warfare are not carnal but mighty through GOD for the pulling down of strongholds. The mind is a battlefield and being able to properly maneuver through emotions helps us to be stable during the fight. The enemy wants to attack and use your emotions to sabotage you, but now you know the game. He will still try to attempt to come for you in every emotion we named and even more but see him with open eyes and defeat him.

Your Sister in LOVE,
Marquetta Marie

Contacts

You can reach Maquetta Marie
On the following Social Media Platforms:

Marquetta Marie (FB)

marquetta_marie_ (IG)

quetta7014@yahoo.com (email)